PARENT ME...
PLEASE!

PARENT ME...PLEASE!
What Teens Have To Say About Good Parenting Will Shock You
Dr. Carol Razza and Denis Eirikis
ISBN: 0-9712299-1-0

Library of Congress Control Number: 2001095073

Book design and layout: Jonathan Gullery

Your comments on this and all other Clear Light publications are welcome. Please
write to the address above or email *feedback@clearlightcoms.com*

To order gift copies of this book please call
Order Hotline 561/793-5222.
Printed in the United States of America

PARENT Me...PLEASE!

What Teens Have To Say About Good Parenting Will Shock You

DR. CAROL RAZZA
and
DENIS EIRIKIS

www.clearlightcoms.com
(561)793-5222

Thanks

This book is dedicated to good parents everywhere who take their responsibilities seriously. This book is especially dedicated to those parents who lead by example, who spend time with their children, who teach them, who respect them, who listen and talk to them, who draw boundaries and give freedom to grow within those bounds, and who know the self-sacrificial nature of what it means to love one's children. Thanks to Ed and Rose, Casper and Elvira.

The co-authors would like to thank all of the kids who responded to our survey and to all of our friends who helped distribute them.

Important Notice

Throughout this book, in order to better illustrate various points, references are occasionally made to case histories of people that Dr. Razza has encountered during her twenty years of family practice. In order to protect anonymity and privacy, names and details have been changed to such an extent, and composite sketches used, to make it absolutely impossible for the reader to identify any particular person.

Any similarity between the fictionalized names and details of people and incidents mentioned in this book and any real people, is not representative of reality, but is in the imagination of the reader.

Contents

Introduction

Parenting Teens Is So Hard... That Nature Usually Requires 12 Years Parenting Experience As A Prerequisite.

Dr. Carol Razza and I think there is great news in this book for parents of teens. The good news is that there are answers, there are solutions, and your teens want to help you find them. The bad news is that parenting always requires hard work.

I wish I had a nickel for every time wiser, more experienced parents cautioned, "Don't worry... it keeps getting harder."

When our three children were infants, I couldn't imagine anything harder than constant diaper changes, colic, sleepless nights, crying, and more diaper changes. I kept waiting for it to get easier.

Later, when they achieved mobility, our rug rats showed great ability to climb and run quickly into trouble. I remember once suggesting to my wife that we build a swimming pool. She said, "How will you keep the kids from drowning in our pool if you can't even keep them out of the toilet?"

Parenting toddlers demands constant vigilance. It required that my wife and I pay more attention to parenting than we had ever paid to anything in our entire lives. How many times do we read in the newspaper that, during a parent's five-minute distraction, the toddler wandered into the pool or into traffic? I kept waiting for it to get easier.

In some ways the elementary years were easier. No more toilet diving. No more worry of blindly following a bouncing ball out into the street. Rather, what became scary was how smart the kids were becoming. They started asking hard questions. "Daddy, did you ever do drugs?" "Daddy, did you ever smoke cigarettes?" "If God made us, then who made God?" "Why do I have to wear a bicycle helmet if you never had to wear one?" "Why are the other kids allowed to stay out late or watch MTV?"

While infancy and the early years were physically demanding, parenting adolescents started to get intellectually challenging. The kids had an awful lot of questions and parenting seemed to demand having lots of right answers.

Then the teen years came. Good thing we already have a dozen solid years of parenting experience under our belts before the firstborn turns into a teenager. My eyes finally became opened to the fact that parenting keeps getting harder rather than easier.

My most valuable insight into adolescence came while teaching Sunday school to a diverse group of 13-year-olds. It was a first-hand glimpse into the gritty world of middle school with its tremendous forces of peer pressure. It was all right there in front of me, in that small class, where I encouraged every child to share openly about their views, their faith, their experiences, and their fears.

In that small group of twenty middle school students, several openly admitted experimenting with drugs, cigarettes, sex and alcohol.

One troubled kid, a rebellious boy who liked to act the role of class clown, shared with me in tears after school one day that his home life was so terrible, and his relationship with his dad was so bad, that he was considering suicide. This same boy, with his hundred dollar sneakers and his "rebellious coolness", seemed to attract a following and I learned that he later successfully encouraged others to experiment with alcohol and drugs. On the outside, the kid seemed to have it all including popularity. But on the inside, he was deeply troubled and had severe scarring from his father.

For the first time, I became aware of what my own middle-schooler faced in the everyday. Middle school is a place where peer pressure and the desire to be popular dominate the child's landscape. Children can be brutally mean to each others' weaknesses. On the first day of seventh grade, my son told me how a group of boys picked on one kid badly in the cafeteria line because he wasn't wearing new sneakers the first day of school. Among their peers, teens have to build defensive mechanisms and remain "on guard." It is crucially important that the home be a safe harbor of affirmation and emotional encouragement where a child can be free to be their natural self.

Gradually, as a parent, it occurred to me that instead of needing my intellectual answers, my children more needed my emotional support. It became clearer that the most valuable things I could give my kids were my time, my love and my acceptance. They didn't need my intellect as much anymore, as their own knowledge started to exceed mine in areas like computers and popular culture. In fact, readers of this book will be struck by the wisdom and intelligence of our teen contributors.

In our modern culture, we know that parenting teens is not easy. In the aftermath of Columbine and other school shootings, no shortage of experts stepped forward to place blame on a wide range of causes including: schools, parents, teachers, and violent entertainment including television, rap music, movies, and video games. It was clear to everyone that something was going wrong in our society and experts from politicians to preachers to PhD's stepped forward to advance their own agendas. But few, however, thought to ask the teens themselves.

In the summer after Columbine, Dr. Carol Razza and I started to discuss doing a book together with the working title, "The Family That Plays Together, Stays Together". We are both true believers that spending a lot of quality time with kids is one of the highest priorities that any parent could have.

To test our theory, we designed an informal survey form that asked kids ages 9-19:

a) "On a scale of 1-10...how would you rank your family's happiness?"

b) "On a scale of 1-10...how often do you play with your parents?"

c) "On a scale of 1-10...how often do you pray with your parents?"

Almost as an afterthought, to see what the teens would say, we decided to add the following question on the survey:

"Dear Student,

The only thing scarier than being a kid or teenager is being the parent of a kid or teenager. Adults forget what it is like to be your age. From your perspective, what are the five most important pieces of advice you can give to any parents trying to have a happy family?"

We distributed the surveys randomly using our network of associates, friends, and relatives across the nation. At the request of our friends who teach in public school systems, we decided to withdraw the question about family prayer.

While we never intended to make this a scientific survey with statistical accuracy, the 1000 teens we surveyed represent a fairly valid cross section of public and parochial school children around the United States. A few of the responses came via the Internet from places including England and Australia.

The wisdom and sincerity of the teen's answers astounded us.

The conventional wisdom of the age drastically differs from what the teens actually told us. For example, anyone watching television or movies would conclude that teens desperately want to spend less time with parents and more time with their friends. **The fact is that the #1 answer teens gave** us is that they desperately want to spend more time with their time-starved parents.

Here is a listing of some of the startling views that teens told us compared with the conventional wisdom of our culture:

Myth: Teens want no discipline
Truth: Teens want clear boundaries and consequences.
Myth: Teens don't want to listen
Truth: Teens want parents to teach them
Myth: Teens want parents to leave them alone.
Truth: Teens want to have fun with parents.

The intelligence and moral maturity of the answers surprised us, but it is the innocent and transparent language of the children that moved our hearts. We created this book so that perhaps their wisdom can move your heart as well.

We organized the thousands of responses into fourteen general categories and we are presenting a representative sampling of them here under self-explanatory chapters.

The co-authors have decided to take a step back and let the teens toss you their pearls of wisdom in their own language. Each chapter ends with the analysis and comments of Dr. Carol Razza, with her twenty years of experience as a licensed family therapist and her nearly thirty years of experience as a parent. They are intended not to take wind from the sails of the teen's comments, but rather to reinforce their positive message and drive the points home in a professional context which parents might find useful.

The comments of the teens themselves are edited only for spelling, not for grammar. We selected about 500 of the most representative comments out of more than 4000 comments received. We tried to avoid repetition.

As we were compiling the comments, we could not help but be struck by their wisdom and purity, and how they tended to echo "traditional family values." The children's advice could just as well have come from grandparents or child development experts. From the transparency of the comments, readers will quickly come to the conclusion that most of the respondents genuinely crave good parenting. Hence our title, "Parent Us...Please!"

The authors make no attempt to statistically analyze the data. Nor do we attempt to interpret the comments. However, we cannot help but to observe that the comments from today's teens represent good news.

Apparently, teens want to communicate with their parents. Teens want their parents to draw boundaries and to create relationships built upon mutual respect and lots of love. Teens want their parents to be the boss. Most of all, parent-starved teens want to spend more time with their time-starved parents.

For parents, this is good news indeed. Teens seem ready and willing to meet parents halfway. It's up to parents to make this happen.

But enough for the introduction. Let's see what the teens themselves and Dr. Razza have to say.

Denis Eirikis

September 2001

Chapter 1

Listen With Your Mind, Heart, And Soul

Listen even if you don't want to.

Talk to your kids and when they talk to you, listen. Listen with your mind, heart, and soul, not just your ears. *girl 14*

I always thought that if a parent pays attention to the kid no matter how stupid the question, it makes us feel loved. *girl 11*

Listen, listen. Listen to your children. They want to know you care about things that happen to them. *girl 14*

Listen even if you don't want to. *girl 14*

Listen to your kids!. They aren't as ignorant as you might think. *boy 18*

Give all family members a chance to express their feelings, all family members' feelings are important. *girl 11*

Make it clear that your children may talk to you about anything. Don't let them ever feel embarrassed to ask you about anything. *girl 19*

Listen to your children. Never disregard anything they say as unimportant. *girl 18*

If we say nothing is wrong or we don't want to talk about it, respect that. Offer to help, offer to be around IF needed, but then back off. Let us come to you if you have already tried coming to us and have been frustrated with the results. *girl 18*

Listen to them and then help them sort out the problem. No need to interrupt them. *girl 16*

Listen to your children. DO Not hear them, actually listen, think about, and put yourself in their position. If you don't listen to them and just hear them, the kids are likely to resent the parents. *boy 15*

Listen to them and make a real effort to take their thoughts into consideration, though they may find this corny and annoying at first, it gets the message across. *boy 15*

Do not hover over your children or nag them or ask them the exact same question over and over, ex.: Everyday my mom comes home and asks: "What's the homework situation." *boy 13*

Always listen to your child if you are uncertain something is wrong. *girl 12*

First of all, the parents need to understand their children, and listen to what they have to say. This would help us teens and pre-teens. *girl 12*

If a kid gets in trouble listen to what they have to say before grounding them. *boy 12*

I can say listen to your children and spend the most amount of time you can with them. *boy 14*

Let your kids talk before you annoy them with all these lectures on how to live. *girl 12*

Always ask your kid their opinion whether you are going to use it or not, they need to feel like they contribute a little. *girl 13*

Listen to your children and what they have to say. Always stay in touch with your children and don't forget about them. *girl 13*

Always listen to your children and never laugh when they are serious, try to remember your needs when you were young and incorporate that into your advice. *girl 12*

Be a good listener and listen whenever he or she tries to talk to you. *boy 12*

Try to understand as much as you can about what your child is saying to you and try to be aware of what he/she is into or what he/she likes to do. *boy 12*

If your child wants to talk, take that time because it won't happen too often. *girl 12*

You have to listen to your children and sincerely listen to their perspective. *boy 12*

NEVER have a heavy discussion, we hate that. Ask them nonchalantly (I hope that's a word) and listen to what they are really saying. *boy 12*

Sit down and have a talk with your family. Find out what they dislike about what you do with them or where you take them. *girl 12*

Always listen first before you talk. *girl 13*

Listen to their story. Don't jump to conclusions. And know all the facts before you start yelling. *boy 13*

Listen more to what your kids have to say and don't say no all the time. *boy 14*

Ask your kids how their day was and start a conversation. *girl 13*

From the Family Therapist

Hundreds of kids all told us variations of the same thing, "Please listen; you are not hearing us. We can't get through and it's so frustrating."

One of my most frustrated and anxious patients was a man approximately 45 years old, who had earned a Ph.D. in engineering. He had worked in his field for about twenty years and hated every minute of it. He could hardly even speak to me without either choking up with tears of confusion or moving about anxiously in his chair during therapy.

I asked what led him to this career, since he obviously hated it. He replied, "It was my dad's dream to become an engineer. The war broke out and my dad had to serve. He never fulfilled his dream, so I had to do it for him."

"I wish he had listened between the lines when I agreed to go to college to complete an advanced degree in engineering. If he had really listened, he would have clearly heard that my passion wasn't for engineering; my passion has always been for music. I tried to tell him this a hundred times, but he just wouldn't listen."

After approximately six months of therapy, he left a very lucrative mechanical engineering career to pursue his dream. He now teaches piano to children by day and plays in a blues band at night.

His decision to leave engineering freed him. Someone had

actually listened.

The quotes we printed in this chapter were only the tip of the iceberg. Almost every teen surveyed repeated the same request, "Please listen to us."

It reminded me of some friends who have a grandfather clock that chimes super-loudly. When I visit, the clock will strike and startle me. The whole house seems to shake. But my friends, who have had the clock for 30 years, don't even hear it. We all learn to tune things out. Many parents have learned to tune out their children.

I once had a teen patient whose mother refused to listen to the dark songs that she wrote. The mother thought that it was a phase and simply refused to listen. As the child became more withdrawn and depressed, the family came to me for counseling and I asked to listen to her songs. They were all about suicide. Anyone who took the time to listen to the lyrics would know that the writer was contemplating suicide. Fortunately, this was years ago and the girl went through counseling and treatment and is now leading a happy life as a young adult. Her mother's failure to listen came very close to tragedy.

Here's the good news. While it's easy to tune your kids out and not pay attention...it's even easier to put down the newspaper, turn off the television, put some time aside and keenly listen to what they have to say.

Listening is the key to every parenting skill. If you don't listen, you might as well ditch all the rest of the advice in this book. Since it's so important, my "tips" section is more detailed here than in the other chapters.

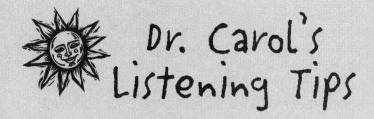

Dr. Carol's Listening Tips

1-Be Present.

Make the choice to be present to your children. One 12 year old girl responded, "Please don't turn anything on while you are listening to us." Imagine trying to share from your heart with your spouse or friend while they look distracted and turn on the TV while you are talking. Being present means putting my needs aside for someone else's needs and listening totally (actively) to the person who is speaking. How? Sometimes we have to prepare ourselves by:

a) Wanting to be present
b) Praying for the strength to put my needs aside for the good of my children.
c) Knowing that what you do today will affect their entire life.

2-Listen Actively.

Use eye contact. Make sure your body language signals receptivity. Nod your head in the affirmative to encourage your teen to say what is on his or her heart. Maintain eye contact, watch your body language, and avoid negative non-verbal responses like shrugs.

3-Listen with respect.

Be kind, loving, and gentle. (We do it for strangers)
No scowling.

4-Don't accuse. Don't jump to conclusions. Listen First.

5-Put time aside each day for each child.

(Fifteen minutes goes a long way)

6-No put downs or condemning statements.

You will get much better results by affirming the positive.

7-Make it Happen.

Be honest, if you can't listen attentively immediately, tell your child how important it is for you to listen and schedule a meeting with them as soon as possible, preferably within the hour.

8-Sometimes Just Listening is Enough.

Listen to all they have to say. Don't try to fix them…help them learn to fix themselves.

9-Be clear.

Let your children know by your words and actions that all that they have to say is important and is worth listening to.

10-Listen to Their Feelings.

Don't minimize your child's feelings by immediately interjecting your own feelings. This sends the message that your feelings are important and your child's feelings are not.

For example:

Teen: "I am frustrated and angry that I can't go to the party because I am grounded."

Mom: "How do you think I felt when you came home late last night? I was scared."

A better approach: "I can understand that you must be angry, I would be too. Let's talk about better ways to keep you from getting grounded again."

11-Don't respond with demands.

Let your child voice his or her concerns, and come up with solutions together. Preferably in collaboration, calmly and rationally set boundaries and consequences.

12-Don't counterattack.

Instead of acknowledging how your child feels, some knee-jerk and respond to their criticism by criticizing them. Consider the outside chance that their criticism has some merit, and respond only after you have calmed down.

13-Don't dredge up past grievances.

Not if you want to hear what they have to say and want them to hear you.

14-No sarcasm.

It's about as unhealthy to communication as throwing acid into the room.

15-Never withdraw love.

Let me repeat this...never ever withdraw your love.

16. Never weary of trying. Keep reminding yourself how important they are.

Chapter 2
Talk To Your Kids!

They usually actually are listening, despite what you may think.

Talk to your kids about important issues. *Girl 16*

Be willing to talk about important things anytime anywhere. *Boy 14*

Always ask your kid how their day was, even if you have not been getting along with them that particular day. *girl 14*

Most importantly talk to your children about ANYTHING! Answer their questions honestly and don't lie. *girl 14*

Talk to your kids!. They usually actually are listening, despite what you may think. *boy 18*

Talk to your kids about friends, boyfriends, etc. but don't be too pushy and persistent. *girl 14*

First and foremost, if we ask you if we can do something, like go out with friends or something, and you want to tell us, "NO" please give us a reason so it can at least be discussed. "Because I said no" is really irritating because we really want to know why. We want to understand you, but if we don't know why you refuse to allow us things, all we can do is get pissed off and then arguments and grudges usually follow. *boy 17*

Talk to your teenager about things that are going on in the world (I.e. Drugs, alcohol, problems like Kosovo, etc. - don't let him/her live a completely sheltered life.) *girl 13*

Talk to them daily. Ask about boyfriends and girlfriends and make sure they aren't doing too much. *girl 13*

Have my dad and I talk more. *girl 13*

Ask them how they're doing in school, etc. and take an interest in what they're doing (within reason, you don't have to start playing computer games, if they start to talk about them, switching off is fine), always let them know if you think they've done something good too. It'll help them to tell you stuff and feel more confident. *boy 15*

Always talk to your child about anything. Make sure that they know that you won't get angry about anything they tell you. *girl 11*

Always talk to your kids over dinner. Ask questions like "How was school?" "Do you need any help with your homework?" or "Anything interesting happened today?" *girl 11*

Another thing is being able to talk to your kids to make sure they are not getting into anything bad and just to see his/her feelings on things. *girl 12*

Always ask your kids how their day was and other questions like that because that will make them feel good. *boy 13*

Talk to your children to see if there is anything wrong or ask them how their day was and have a conversation with them. *girl 13*

If somebody has a problem, offer them advice it may come in handy. *girl 12*

Support each other and when they ask a question answer them because lots of times there's only a couple of questions that we kids ask. *girl 11*

Talk them at night about school & how their day went.
girl 12

Kids should be able to talk to their parents without feeling embarrassed or without their mom or dad making them feel uncomfortable. *girl 11*

Talk to your kids and when they talk to you...listen. Listen with your mind, heart, AND SOUL, NOT JUST YOUR EARS. *girl 14*

Discuss problems with your child, do not shout or lecture on and on and on. *girl 14*

I think parents should talk to their kids or teenagers, like they are one of their own friends. That eases the tension and nervousness sometimes. *girl 12*

Have a conversation with each individual daily. *girl 13*

They shouldn't repeat things more than twice to get their point across, believe me, we hear them. *girl 13*

Great conversations... no yelling. No screaming. *boy 13*

Say goodnight before they go to bed. *girl 14*

Say goodbye before they go to bed. *boy 14*

I think they should sit down every night and talk about their days. *girl 14*

From the Family Therapist

Wow! So our teens do want us to talk to them. But what do they want us to say?

Parents have wisdom, experience and hope to share with children. Think of how you have learned from your experiences and from those you respect. Try to pass that knowledge down to your children.

Many of my patients had their parents constantly preach to them, instead of talking to or sharing with them. "Do as I say and not as I do"… is all too common.

I had a fifteen-year-old patient who said that the only things she ever heard from her parents were yelling, shouting, preaching and condemning. Simple and cordial conversation became rare. The more the parents dug their heels in and shouted and ordered her around, the more the girl dug her heels in and rebelled. In her case, the reason she rebelled was in an attempt to "get even" with her parents for all of the hard feelings that their shouting and condemnation had caused her. The way she rebelled was to go against the teachings and moral beliefs of her parents and so she became active in drugs, crime, and promiscuity.

Many parents who constantly preach and harp on their teens think they are "talking with them." Remember how easy it is for you to tune our teens out? Parental preaching and whining is the guaranteed best way to teach your teens to tune you out.

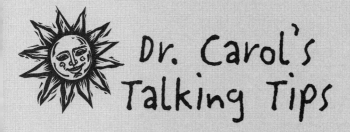

Dr. Carol's Talking Tips

1. I believe that the truth sets us free. Answer your teen's tough questions honestly. For example, many Baby Boomer parents experimented with drugs. Don't glamorize. Stress any consequences you faced as a result of your behavior that you do not want your teens to face.
2. Work on yourself. Until you are comfortable with who you are, in light of your past, you will have a hard time sharing without either glamour to make it seem alright, or dishonestly because of shame.
3. Preaching is not talking. Most of us will not come back for a second conversation if the first interaction was one-sided. Leave preaching for the pulpit. Speak with your heart and listen and respond lovingly to what comes back.
4. Practice listening skills. Kids will respond to conversation if they know they are being heard.
5. Don't interrogate. Leave that for the sheriff. Using good listening skills will reap you better information about what's going in your teen's life.
6. Don't Condemn. This is a roadblock to beneficial communication.

The best words you can say to your kids are: "I love you just the way you are."

Chapter 3

Spend Time Together

Every Step Of The Way... Be There!

Spend a lot of time with your children. *Girl 16*

Be involved, volunteer in their school, etc. *girl 16*

Be there. Every step of the way... be there. Every little thing... be there, because it is important. *boy 19*

Make sure your family spends time together. This is especially important when your children are young. *boy 18*

Try to spend quality time, but don't try to be "cool"(as you parents think) because then parents will just embarrass or drive their kids away, try like, a family dinner every week... not a movie, something that requires the family to talk. *boy 15*

Try participating in anything you can to help your child, like homework, help them practice for something, etc. *boy 15*

Tell them you will always be there for them even when you are dead and mean it. *boy 15*

Stay active in their lives. *girl 16*

Spend a little bit of time with them. *boy 14*

Always give attention to your kid. *boy 13*

The family should set some dates to have a family dinner. This would be a time to find out what's been going on at your children's school. *girl 12*

The parents should spend time with their children. But the parent should NEVER treat their kids differently this would only make the other children jealous and upset. *girl 12*

Make sure you have time for your kids, pay attention to their problems. *girl 11*

Go to their activities to support their interests by educating yourself about them. Then you can participate and know what's going on. *girl 14*

If you work a lot still try to find time to spend with us. *girl 14*

You need to spend more time with your children and talk to them about important things like drugs, sex, violence, etc. Be like their friend and respect their feelings when they talk to you about that stuff. *boy 15*

Never stop checking up on your children even if they are generally a good kid. *girl 13*

Never assume you know your children, because usually not even they do. *girl 13*

Try to be interested in their hobbies because your hobbies are not what they like. *boy 13*

Come to your children's activities such as a soccer game or piano recital. *girl 13*

You should let them help you in the kitchen making dinner or lunch. *girl 13*

Try and be interested in something your children likes and you can share that with your child and you will have a better relationship. *boy 12*

Give your child a lot of attention because all kids like attention. *boy 12*

Bond with them, we really like to be able to spend time together with parents. *girl 12*

You have to spend time with your family members to get closer to them. *girl 12*

Make sure the child knows that you are there for help and if he seems to not be acting normal, ask if anything is wrong, then listen. *boy 12*

Always say goodnight. *girl 11*

You need to make sure that they're spending enough time with their kids and the dads don't just think about work. *girl 11*

To make sure they are always there for you when you need advice or help without laughing or making you feel bad. *girl 11*

Tell them you will always be there and they'll have someone to talk to in times of need. *boy 12*
Make them feel comfortable with you so that if ever they have a problem, they can come to you for help. *girl 12*

Parents should spend more time with kids instead of with TV. *boy 12*

Make them go to work with you at least 2 times a year so you can show them how hard it is. *girl 12*

You should not leave your boy or girl all the time. *boy 11*

Spend as much time with them as possible, you don't know what the next day brings. *girl 14*

Put your kids before you. *boy 13*

Stay in your kid's life. *boy 13*

Try to act interested in our life, but not over-interested. *girl 13*

We rarely do anything, or have fun as a family. When it's just my mom and I we do fun things. It's not often that my dad and I even talk. Which is stupid because we all live together. *girl 13*

Spend as much time as possible with them.. They need love. *boy 13*

Make sure that your kid's friends are not bad role models. *boy 14*

 # From the Family Therapist

There is a natural collision course taking place in our culture. Time-starved parents are creating parent-starved children.

Parents: It is important for you to reflect back on a few questions from your own childhood:

- When you were a kid, who was there for you, really there for you? Was there someone that you could always count on and you knew it?
- What did you learn?
- Did the security of having someone to count on help make you a better person?
- Now think about the opposite. Do you remember a time or times in your life when you felt needy and you counted on someone who really wasn't there for you? Was there someone who refused to make the time for you or let you down in some way? Get back into the skin of that child...how did it make you feel? What did this rejection tell you about yourself? Did it do anything good for your self-esteem? Did it affect the formation of who you are today?

"Every step of the way be there," doesn't mean pick up the pieces for them or take away their natural consequences. It means being there for all the big and little things. Just be there!

Spend as much time as possible with them. They need your love. A good parent puts your child's needs before your own. Something that the "me generation" often has a hard time doing. All the kids are asking for is a parent's attention. If the parent won't pay attention, then who will?

My own son was about 12 when I opened my family therapy practice. I found myself making appointments with clients morning, noon, and night. I was excited and felt important with so many patients relying upon me. One night when I was leaving for a group therapy session, when I kissed my son goodbye, he said, " Mom, you never have any time for us anymore." I was shocked back to reality. I dropped everything, cancelled all of my evening commitments, and got back to being mom first. It's a decision I never regretted.

I know this is not politically correct, however, I really don't care. Dads, you are the protectors of that family, the Godly leader. Protecting not only physically, keeping a roof over their heads but also, emotionally— teaching them, loving them, caring for them, guiding them. What messages are we giving our children if as parents we are not available to them?

Tell them you will always be there and they'll have someone to talk to in times of need. How can you make time for business, for friends, for golf, for television…while denying your teen your positive attention?

Moms, most of you already know to the core how important motherhood is. Our children are young for only a short time in our lives. In my twenty years experience as a family therapist, I can assure you that having a parent home when a kid comes home from school makes a huge difference in their lives. Be there for them.

I remember one family that would walk on pins and needles when dad was home. There were only certain times he would make himself available to the children. TV sports were dad's highest priority. If a game was on TV, then kids were prohibited from approaching him. No one was allowed to make noise or even ask a homework question. Of course, when his children grew up they didn't want to have anything to do with their father even though by this point he had drastically changed his ways. It reminds me of the song, "Cats in the Cradle."

I remember the pain on the face of a dad whose teen son was killed in an auto accident. The son had asked the dad desperately to come with him to a school function, one that the father thought of as useless. The teen died on the way home. Fifteen years later, the dad is still haunted by the "what ifs."

I can tell immediately how a family interacts at home as they enter into my office. Who sits next to who and body language speak volumes. When families spend time together, they become comfortable with one another, more sensitive to one another's needs. You can see it and feel it.

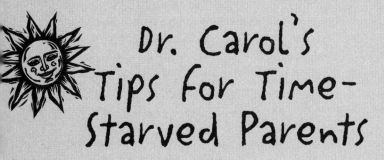

Dr. Carol's Tips for Time-Starved Parents

- Parents will either make time happen or not. Kids don't want to hear our stories of woe. "I can't make it to your baseball game because I am working to give you a better life." A "better life" is being at the baseball game!
- You will know your kids better if you spend time sharing every aspect of their lives…not just homework or chores. Know their friends, teachers, and coaches.
- Be involved. Volunteer at school or as a coach.
- Schedule family time each week. Put dates with your kids in a planner and treat them as important appointments.
- Don't break appointments with your kids any more than you would break important appointment with your boss or best client.
- There is no way to "make time". No way to get 25 hours into a day. The only way time with your kids is going to happen is if you take the time from something else.

Time with your family will only happen if you schedule it.

Chapter 4
Play With Us

At times just go and do fun things and forget about being a parent

Take a day off to be with them (on the weekend most likely.)
girl 14

Do things with them as a family and make sure they feel special. *boy 16*

If your kid finishes his/her homework for the first time in a month, he/she has been so busy, don't say you can't play basketball. *girl 11*

Parents should plan to take off a certain day from work and go fishing with their son or just play around with the kids. *boy 11*

Always play with your child if they say that they are bored.
girl 12

Go on a lot of vacations to get away from things that you don't like, ex: work, school. *girl 12*

Use family activities to open any closed lines of communication you may have with your child. *boy 12*

Have fun together. *boy 19*

Do what your kids want to do such as if your daughter wants to give you a make-over let her, if they want to play a board game play it with them or if they want to drive the lawn mower teach them how. *boy 12*

Parents should make one day of the week to play a game with the whole family. *girl 12*

You could have a family day and spend what everyone likes to do and take turns picking. *girl 10*

You should try to play as much as possible with each other. *boy 11*

Don't spend your free time gossiping with friends, go on a nice picnic with your family. *girl 11*

Families should take the time to do things together...they aren't going to be together forever. *girl 11*

If you are not busy, always try to do things with them. Play basketball or go for a walk. *girl 13*

Try to find something your child likes to do that is not with their friends and try to do it with them or help find out stuff etc. and do it with them. *boy 13*

Go places where you went when you were little. *girl 12*

Spend a lot of time with your kids, go places, don't ignore them. *girl 12*

Don't let them feel left out, do activities with them and play with them. *boy 13*

You can do family activities like going to the beach, mall, movies, or over friends house. *girl 12*

Take your kids to the beach, play catch with them, and ask them to teach you how to surf. *boy 12*

Parents should spend more time with their kids and play games, go to the beach or movies because sometimes all kids want is a little attention. *girl 13*

At times just go and do fun things and forget about being a parent. *girl 11*

Play with your kid at least 2 1/2 hours a day. *girl 11*

Don't forget you can play video games with your kids. *boy 12*

Take your family outings on weekends to bring you closer together. *girl 13*

Look for things that are going on in your town in the newspaper so there's something to do on weekends. *boy 14*

From The Family Therapist

In the military, under penalty of court martial, officers are prohibited from "fraternizing" with the enlisted. The theory is that if the enlisted person is allowed to see the humanity of the officers, then strict military discipline and the blind obedience to orders will break down.

This is an effective leadership style if the object of the game is to ensure that an otherwise sane 18 year old will blindly follow orders into harm's way.

Too many parents, especially fathers, bring this standoffish leadership style to the family table.

Families aren't places where a parent must feel that he or she must wear a mask of authority. Parents should set the example by being themselves. A healthy home is the only safe place that allows a teen to be who they are at the core. The home should be a safe nurturing environment where everyone can simply be themselves and no one has to take on a false persona.

I am not suggesting that you do not accept parental responsibilities and assert authority; rather this chapter is about the need for kids to occasionally play with the *real* you. In my twenty years of experience, I have found that playing with kids results in less rebellious behavior.

For example, many of my patients were brought up under "drill sergeant" dads. This type of authority figure begs for open and dramatic rebellion.

In reality, moms and dads who let their hair down and play like one of the kids actually tend to encourage and attract even more love and respect from teens.

Some parents think that taking their kids to organized sports practice is the same thing as playing with their kids. Competitive sports put pressure on the kid to succeed. It's a place where they have to put on a public persona and perform to please mom and dad.

Don't get me wrong. Competitive sports aren't bad. But the therapeutic and playful interaction that I especially encourage between parents and teens cannot be achieved with you in the stands and them on the field.

Families benefit from connecting. I strongly recommend that parents let their hair down often and simply play with their kids. I am not talking about sports or competition so much as simple, creative play.

The very best kind of family play doesn't involve competition so much as it involves providing a safe, fun, no-pressure way to interact as a family.

Dr. Carol's Tips on Family Play

- The more you connect when they are younger, the less likely you are to have rebellious teen strangers, instead of loving teenaged children, living under your roof.
- Schedule Family nights where everyone can let their guard down.
- Consider dressing up for family meetings...either in formal attire or even in makeshift costume.
- Encourage joyful playful behavior. It's therapeutic.
- Enjoy your kids and forget "what are people going to say?"
- Downplay competition. Put on family skits. Make a video together. Play music together. Jump in puddles.
- Start a family arts and crafts night. Lego's are great. I also recommend playing with clay. You would be delightfully surprised to see how therapeutic and enriching this activity can be.
- My personal favorite is playfully fighting it out with water pistols or foam sponge balls. I know it sounds terrible, but after an aerobic family play session of zinging foam balls, my family collapses together in laughter and hugs.

Chapter 5

Love

Always love them....and harder.

Always love them. And harder, always show your love for them. *boy 19*

Tell your kids how important and loved they are EVERY day. *boy 18*

Love us. It may not always be easy, but tell us you love us, too, as much as we manage to only mumble a response, we need and love to hear it. And we love you too. *boy 17*

Don't be afraid to say, "I love you." *boy 14*

Make your kids feel important and always hug them and tell them you love them, even if you think, "oh they know I love them". Trust me they need the reinforcement, to know someone loves them. *girl 14*

Of course love your children. *boy 16*

Be a friend to your kids, not just a parent. *girl 14*

Don't tell them that you don't love them. *boy 13*

If I were a parent I would always show love and interest in what my kid is doing. *boy 13*

Show them you care (come to a sports game or play.) *girl 15*

Show your love to your child and children so they should show love to their parents. *girl 11*

Always love your child and give hugs to him or her every day. *boy 11*

Give more hugs. *boy 11*

Well, we should love each other even if we do something wrong. *girl 12*

Parents should spend as much time with their children as possible and always tell them they love them. *girl 11*

Hug your children often and show them affection. Then they will love also. *girl 14*

Tell your family and your child that you love them. Hug them and give them a kiss at night or when they are leaving to go somewhere. Show them you love them. *boy 14*

Always tell your kids that you love them. Make sure every time your child needs you, you will try to be there. *girl 13*

Be loving so the kids will be loving to other people. *girl 12*

To love your kids unconditionally, no matter what they do or say always love them even though you may not always like them. *girl 14*

Kids love to tell their parents that they love you but sometimes they say it when your parents are mad at you or something and they don't tell you how much they love you even if you did something wrong. *girl 14*

Parents should always love their kids even if they get in trouble or get bad grades. *boy 12*

Hug them as many times as you can. *boy 13*

From The Family Therapist

Love is such an easy word to throw around. People *love* baseball and they *love* chocolate cake. The type of love that a parent needs to show to a child is a deeply unconditional love.

I had a patient whose mother always told her, "I love you, but if you ever get pregnant I will throw you out on the street and never speak to you again in my life."

Of course, where do you think the daughter looked for unconditional love? That's right, straight into the arms (and bed) of the first teenaged boy who told her he loved her no matter what.

The very worst thing parents can do is to withhold love or affection. That's as cruel and senseless as withholding food and nourishment from a baby.

I heard one lovely young woman interviewed on television who was part of a chastity movement. She said that one of the things that helped in her goal of abstaining from sex before marriage was her loving and nurturing parents who hugged and kissed her goodnight and who often said, "I love you."

Affection is important, but unconditional love is crucial. Never give your child the message that, "I will love you IF you do this, or IF you don't do that."

We all need love and affection. If teens don't get love and affection at home, then they will seek it someplace else.

Tips for Unconditional Love

- Look beyond your children's behavior. No one said we have to love poor or sinful choices, just our kids.
- Know that if you love and respect them...they will learn to love and respect themselves.
- Don't take things so personally. When kids act up, parents have a tendency to believe, "If they loved me, they wouldn't do that." When, in reality, we have to help them love themselves.
- Help them to realize that they are beautiful gifts.
- Even if your children are teenagers, start a nightly ritual of "tucking them in." Kiss and hug them good night and remind them that you love them just the way they are.

Chapter 6
Do As I Say, Not As I Do

Always Lead By Example...

Not By Dictatorship

Don't take kid's money unless you really need it. *boy 12*

Don't set bad examples. *girl 12*

Lead by example not by dictatorship. *boy 18*

First I think to have a happy family, you must love yourself before you can love others. Second make sure you and your partner have a trusting relationship. *girl 12*

Be careful what you say and do. *boy 12*

Father, don't cheat on your wife. *boy 12*

Be a good influence for your kids. *boy 11*

Make sure parents are in agreement about such things as discipline, curfew, rules. Do not let it happen that a child can go against one parent because the other parent says something is ok. *girl 19*

Not overwhelm us with their problems. *girl 13*

Be real. If you are having a rough patch in your marriage don't hide it- kids learn from your mistakes. *boy 19*

Do not get divorced, especially if your parents got divorced. It will scare your children into thinking it's hereditary. And they will not have much of a clue about being a father if they had no father. *boy 19*

Love each other as well. *boy 17*

If you split up then think of the children, no matter how strong they are. It will affect them all their lives. *boy 16*

Stand up to the child. Show them that you are the adult. *girl 12*

If there is a bad (naughty) show on and the kids can't watch it, the parents shouldn't watch either. *girl 11*

Don't cuss around your children, this will only let them think this is allowed, and will do this quite often. *girl 12*

If you and your spouse are going to have a fight, talk instead of yelling. *girl 12*

Do not fight with your spouse in front of your kids, they might think it's OK to do that if you do that. *girl 14*

Don't blame things from the past on your children. *girl 14*

Don't make promises you can't keep. *girl 14*

Make sure you do not do things now if you don't want your kids to follow. *girl 13*

Make sure when you marry someone you truly love him/her so you don't go behind their back and divorce them. *girl 13*

Just remember why we are here and try to get away from your problems. *boy 13*

If you get divorced, stay good friends with your ex. This will help your kids a lot. *boy 13*

You should not act like them. *boy 13*

Act more like a teenager than an older person. *girl 13*

Father, if your wife is going to have a baby don't get divorced. *boy 12*

Father, don't get drunk too often. *boy 12*

If you're frustrated and mad don't blame your kids, just calm down. *girl 12*

To have a right amount of kids cause if you have a lot you might go crazy. *girl 12*

If you are in a pissy mood… don't take it out on someone else. *girl 12*

What you do and say is what your kid's going to do. *girl 13*

Don't get a divorce. *girl 13*

Don't say bad words so they don't become potty mouths. *girl 13*

Be calm if your ideas are not working, then you need to give them more information. *boy 13*

Show that you (the parents) love each other. *girl 13*

Don't become a workaholic. *girl 13*

Practice what you preach. *girl 15*

The first thing that you need is a good, respectful, and nice father to have a happy family. *girl 14*

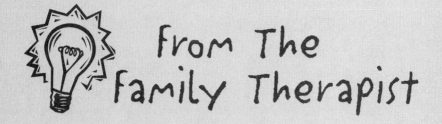

From The Family Therapist

The only effective way to lead your teens is by your example. It's true what they say about actions being louder than words.

How many of us smoke, while we tell the kids not to smoke. If a child hears around the house that his or her parents are cheating on taxes or business expenses, then naturally the child is going to assume that it's OK to cheat, steal, or lie at school.

Fact is, that no matter what you try to teach....if you smoke then your kids are more likely to be smokers. If you fasten your seatbelt, then your teens are more likely to fasten theirs. If you get drunk a lot or sleep around... then it's likely that your children will eventually do the same.

No need for a whole lot of rocket science analysis from the professional therapist, we parents simply need to lead by good example.

I knew a father in New England who was asked by his employer to falsify a report. The father refused to lie and lost his job. He had five school-aged children.

It turned out to be a beautiful thing. Instead of tearing the family apart, the ensuing poverty brought the family together. The three oldest sons all went to work in delicatessens and the money they brought home went to pay the mortgage and the bills. Now, these twenty some years later, the family is still together and they own a chain of successful deli's.

If you set an example of honesty and integrity, love and compassion, then these things will take deep root in your children.

Dr. Carol's
Tips

- Know yourself! Take a critical look. Conduct a dispassionate personal inventory. Don't condemn yourself. Try to learn about your behaviors that need to be strengthened or worked on without self-condemnation. Your job is to be the best parent you can be.
- Try not to rationalize, "I am the adult." Work on changing the behaviors that you do not want to teach your children.
- Ask yourself, "Am I expecting more from my child than I expect of myself?"
- Do I practice what I preach? Do I walk the walk on a regular basis...or merely talk the talk?
- Kids are pretty smart. They know what an imposter is. Don't be one.

Chapter 7

Ritual

Eat Dinner Together

Get out an hour every night to be together. *boy 12*

Do something together at least once a week. Dinner together, family movie or go somewhere. *girl 12*

Eat dinner together and talk about what happened to you in school or at work. *girl 12*

The family should have a time to be together, such as everyone going out to dinner or just being at home. *girl 11*

Every night get together in one room and thank God for each other. Pray and talk about what you like about the other and what you think they can improve without being mean. *girl 11*

Eat dinner together and talk about your day. *boy 10*

Make dinner and have that meal be your family time. It is very important that you spend time with your children and let them know that you care what is going on with them. *girl 14*

Have one night a family night. *boy 13*

The family should try to have family meals at least twice a week. *girl 12*

Have family meetings and have a family night to watch a movie. *girl 12*

Take one day out of the week to go somewhere with your child. Then keep doing that, it makes them feel wanted. *girl 12*

Have a family show that you watch all together. *girl 12*

Have a family night where you sit down and play games. *girl 11*

Family should have a day of the week where they spend quality time together. *girl 12*

From The Family Therapist

There is a commercial on television lately that urges families to eat dinner together once a week. My reaction is one of sadness that, for so many families, dinner together once per week would be an improvement.

It's helpful to remember back to the rituals of your own childhood and how important they were when you were growing up. Most of us have fond memories of Birthdays as milestones to mark the way. Most families ritualistically celebrate holidays whether it's hanging the same Christmas stocking in the same place each year or lighting the Hanukah Menorah that has been passed down from generation to generation.

Everyday rituals are just as important. You can hear the teens ask for some sort of predictability with their requests for family meetings, family meals, and family nights.

Imagine the message it sends, even to teens, when parents come into the room "to tuck them in" at night. A good night kiss, prayer time, and hug is an important part of a child's emotional development. It daily sends them the clear messages: "You are precious," and "You are loved".

Children thrive on ritual. It's a way for parents to pass down love, grace, and tradition. It provides families with an important sense of connectedness, part of a greater whole.

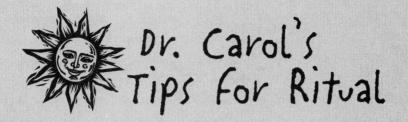

Dr. Carol's Tips for Ritual

- Remember that consistency helps children feel safe.
- Give yourself credit for what you already do. Recognize that ritualizing something means repeating it. For example, in our house Spaghetti and Meatballs on Sunday is a constant. If Sunday passes without it, we all feel like we missed out on something and usually go into withdrawal by Tuesday.
- Consider starting new family traditions even if it is something as simple as returning to a favorite arts festival or sporting event together each year.
- It's sometimes helpful to ritualize in order to break down barriers to communication. For example, consider establishing a special place for important family meetings whether it's a certain room in the house, a place in the backyard, or a picnic table under an oak at a nearby park.
- Our family has a favorite movie. We all watch it, laugh at it, and even repeat the lines together. What movie? FATSO with Dom DeLuise. (grin)
- Some families make a ritual out of everyone being there together with popcorn or snacks for a favorite weekly television show.
- The bottom line is that consistency helps kids and the best kinds of rituals are ones that make them feel important and connected.

Chapter 8

Trust

Trust The Job You Have Done With Us, Let Us Make And Learn From Our Mistakes.

Trust us. *girl 13*

Try not to say anything or do anything to embarrass them in public. Instead, make up a secret sign between you and them to do when you want to hug or kiss them or whatever. *boy 11*

Learn to trust your children. We all do things we later regret, but I think our intentions are almost always good. *boy 18*

Give us space, trust the job you have done with us, let us make and learn from our mistakes. *girl 18*

Let me trust you not to embarrass our friends. *boy 17*

Don't assume that just because your kid is a teen, means they're always trying to do something sneaky. *girl 14*

Don't snoop through their stuff trying to find something you more than likely won't. *girl 14*

Most girls know how to stick up for themselves and say "NO" to guys, just because we go out with guys to the movies, etc. doesn't mean we're going to do anything steamy. *girl 14*

Don't worry so much. The world isn't as wild as you think it is. *boy 15*

Above all, trust is paramount. I have a friend who basically hates his dad and blames most of the rows that go on in his house on his dad. He always has to respect him and can't even give friendly jokes punches or tickle his dad without getting yelled at. His dad also just doesn't trust him, for example: if he goes on the internet while his dad isn't at home he gets shouted at, simply because his dad doesn't trust him with it. Incidentally, he was also grounded for two weeks for a bad report from school. His parents gave no advice or anything to help him. Funnily enough, his dad is an educational psychologist. *boy 15*

Trust your children, many parents don't do it, but try it, it works. *girl 18*

Try not to embarrass your child. *girl 12*

Don't take your kid's things or embarrass them in public. (No inside jokes.) *girl 11*

Give them a chance to prove themselves. *boy 13*

Never embarrass your child in front of other kids, because that's probably why they have bad attitudes with you. *girl 12*

Parents must never lie to their children; this will only hurt them and lead them on to doing things. *girl 12*

Don't embarrass them in front of their friends. *boy 12*

I think you should be able to trust your kids because if you are not able to trust them then they won't get to see how life works and learn responsibility. *girl 12*

Do not embarrass me at any mall!!! *girl 13*

If any of my friends come over, don't show my baby pictures. *girl 13*

Be honest, if everyone isn't your family will tear apart. *girl 13*

When they want to go to the movies by themselves or with friends, don't sit next to them in the theatre. *boy 13*

Be open. Don't hold important things back. They will be more open with you. *girl 13*

Don't be a nerd parent. Where you embarrass your child and do things you don't think you should do. Try to wear clothes that your kids think look good (unless they are bizarre.) *girl 13*

Trust us, we don't lie as much as you think. *girl 13*

Trust them and talk to them. Use them as a friend and not just as a son or daughter. *girl 13*

Be truthful to your child and he or her will learn to respect you for that. *boy 12*

Let them know they can trust you with anything. *boy 12*

Please don't brag about us, we are not that great and neither is the braggart. *girl 12*

Trust them and they'll trust you. *boy 13*

Never make kids keep secrets from the other parent unless it is a surprise party or something. *girl 11*

Trust your children more…but not a lot. *boy 12*

Well I think parents should trust their kids but also look after them and don't totally let them out of your control but also respect the kid. *girl 13*

Don't embarrass them, its very hard being a cool teenager. *girl 14*

Please just trust your child. They are always listening even when you think they aren't. *girl 13*

You should be straight up with your kids and not top the facts with untruths to make it sound better. *boy 12*

When we tell you or mom something, don't blab it off to relatives…you know girl talk. *girl 12*

Trust is very important once you know they trust them they will feel more secure. *girl 12*

Don't pretend to like our music, clothes, etc. Just tell us.
girl 12

Try to have an honest and open relationship with your kids.
Start from when they are young. *girl 12*

Trust before you doubt. *boy 14*

From The Family Therapist

Notice how nicely the teens bring home the point that "Trust" is a two way street. " Please trust us not to do the wrong thing." "We want to trust you not to embarrass us or otherwise hurt us."

All healthy relationships, especially ones between family members, are built upon trust.

Teens will often not live up to the expectations that parents have in mind. Yes, your teen might make a mistake and stray beyond the boundaries you set, but it is an absolute parental disaster to say, "I will never trust you again."

If you find yourself feeling this way, find something, even a little thing, in your child that you can trust. In family counseling, I often recommend this. If trust is to be rebuilt, and family life is unbearable without it, then start with something as simple and predictable as trusting your child to brush his or her teeth.

In less drastic cases, parents will often say things like, "I can't trust my teen to cut the grass even though it's the only job he has in this house."

Yes, there should be consequences, but when you keep sending the child the message, "I can't trust you"…it doesn't help anything but rather becomes a self-fulfilling prophecy.

One sure way to create an untrustworthy child is to keep telling them that they are untrustworthy.

If we keep our children on too short a leash, then we are failing to teach them the critical thinking skills they will need as adults. The children may grow up to be indecisive, neurotically afraid of making decisions, and live in the shadows of fear and doubt.

While some parents fantasize about having 100% faithfully obedient children that never take risks or stray past the boundaries... normal children are not supposed to do this. The developing child is forever exploring envelopes. The last thing you want to produce is a blindly obedient adult who never takes initiative.

Dr. Carol's Tips on Mutual Trust

- Never tell your teen that you will never trust them again.
- Find small things to trust and build from there. You can start by trusting your child to act like the teenager that they are.
- Act as a good role model for trust by trying NOT to embarrass your child or otherwise encouraging them not to trust you.
- Encourage trust by always affirming when your kids make good choices. Avoid diminishing their good deeds by saying, like some parents, "Well, you are supposed to be doing that anyway."
- Laying a foundation of mutual trust can only be done one small stone at a time. If trust has broken down, don't expect to rebuild it overnight. It's hard patient work.

Chapter 9
Teach Your Children

Help Them Achieve Things That Cannot Be Achieved Without a Parent's Help

We think we know it all but you know we don't. Try to teach us in a nice way, use friendly reminders. *boy 12*

Teach them discipline and to be responsible. E.G. To be responsible let them solve their own problems once in a while instead of jumping right into it and solving it for them. *girl 12*

Teach your children respect starting from birth. *girl 16*

Don't be too sensitive, teens in particular tend to get "anti-parent" for a while, but it's normal and will pass. Understand that we need to dislike your rules and your efforts to know us in depth because we don't even know ourselves that well yet. *girl 18*

If your kid gets in trouble, no matter how bad, try to understand. *boy 15*

Be supportive where possible. *boy 17*

Teach them things; tell them about devils like the Trench Coast Mafia. *boy 15*

Encourage your children in their hobbies and activities, don't discourage their hopes of achieving new heights. *boy 15*

Teach your children to respect you from the time they are born. *girl 18*

Get your children into sports and activities while they're young. They'll appreciate it when they get older. Just don't be too pushy about them staying in that activity or sport. *girl 16*

Tell them life is not fair. *boy 9*

Offer encouragement but don't put a lot of pressure on them. *girl 11*

Encourage them but don't push them. *boy 12*

You have to let your kids grow up. Don't try to protect them from everything you think is bad. Tell them when you think it is a bad situation and tell your opinion. *girl 12*

Take time to explain to your kids what things are wrong and what is right. *boy 12*

I think parents should not let kids watch as much of the shows they watch today. Some kids might think it is cool to shoot a gun and then they do it. *girl 12*

If you think that your children or child is doing something don't yell at them so that they get it right just tell them. *girl 12*

If kids get bad grades don't yell at them. Try and help them out. *boy 12*

Don't make your kid feel like a complete loser when they bring home bad grades. *girl 12*

Always forgive your kids if you and they have a fight. Ask them to forgive you. *girl 10*

Parents should take the time to help with homework because they always say education is soooo important. *girl 11*

Read with me *boy 10*

Get a dog and share responsibility. *boy 11*

Help your child with homework and play with them and pray together every day. *girl 13*

Teach your children always to use manners and to be kind to other people. *girl 13*

Always have them involved in some extra-curricular activity, preferably sports so they can learn to be around people and exercise. *girl 12*

Talk about different situations your child could get into with friends or people on the street. *girl 11*

Talk to your kid about their friends and how their friends treat them. *girl 11*

Always accept their apology if they did something wrong. *boy 12*

When doing something for their benefit, tell them that you are not just being mean. *boy 12*

Don't make them unappreciated, encourage them, say you love them. *boy 13*

Give your child a lot of encouragement in what they like to do most. *girl 12*

Tell them to always try to think positively, not negatively. *girl 12*

Reward them for their good tasks and tell them you're proud. *girl 12*

Pressure your kids into sports. *boy 12*

Never send your child to bed without dinner. *boy 12*

Teach them what it's like to be adult. Let them show you what it is like to be a kid. *boy 12*

If somebody's having problems, call a family meeting and talk about it. *girl 12*

Give us 100% encouragement to do good and succeed in everything. *girl 11*

Teach them respect and do things with them. Don't let them slip away. *girl 14*

Encourage your kids not be shy, no one made any friends that way. *girl 12*

Most important, let them fall. And don't cover for them. They need to learn how to face the world. Along with responsibility come choices. And we are not all perfect. But our failures make us stronger. *girl 14*

Get them a pet like a dog, not a stupid pet like a bird or cat. *boy 12*

If your kids make "A's" and "B's" and then gets a "C" on a progress report, just let it slip but if it happens twice then you have a problem. *girl 12*

Enjoy the fun times and grow strong with the bad times. *girl 12*

Let us be kids. Of course we are going to goof sometimes, so don't ground us for acting silly. Compromise more often and don't just yell. *girl 12*

When kids get bad grades or deal with school problems, try hardest to comfort and help the child. *girl 12*

Be both, a parent and a best friend, they need someone to talk out all-important things. Try to be there for them all the time. *girl 14*

Don't focus on only negative things with your kids. *girl 13*

Compliment, recognizing what your kids are doing right. *girl 13*

Be proud of them no matter what. *girl 15*

Don't do things for them that you can do for yourselves. *girl 13*

Help them achieve things that cannot be achieved without parent's help. *girl 13*

Stand by their side if someone accuses them of something. *girl 13*

From The Family Therapist

Once again, the teens said it all. "Teach us the things that we can only learn from a parent." Wow!

I met a woman once who was a schoolteacher. She had several children with a husband who was an abusive alcoholic. It doesn't take a brain surgeon to know that having a drunk and abusive dad, even if he has been asked to move from the house, is the perfect recipe for messing up the life of any child.

This woman couldn't change her husband, but instead she put her effort into being the best mother-teacher she could to her children. This woman spent a lot of time with her children, connecting with them, encouraging them, opening up doors to learning adventure for them, and being extremely sensitive to the children's needs. Thanks to her teaching instincts, her kids grew up to be emotionally healthy young adults.

A common thread that runs through so many of the teen's comments is that they need a parent's encouragement. It's trite but true, that our job is to try to teach and encourage our children to be all that they can be. We don't need to teach them specific tasks so much as to teach them to reach for the stars.

Dr. Carol's Teaching Tips

- The more parents encourage their children's giftedness, the more the children recognize they are gifted. The more gifted they believe themselves to be, the more they will stretch and grow.
- What behavior or attitude do you find most annoying in your child? You will probably get a clue about their giftedness there. For example, if your child can sit endlessly in front of a screen playing computer games, they probably have an aptitude for computer programming or other productive tasks that involve long hours at the computer screen. A child that is strong willed may be a natural leader.
- Teach at their age level. Ask questions to give you an idea of how well they are absorbing what you are teaching.
- Teach by your example. Your actions speak volumes.
- Don't push your kids to learn…encourage them to develop a love of learning.
- Don't be afraid of their questions. Kids learn by asking questions. If you don't know the answer, help them find it online or in a library.

Chapter 10

Respect: The Golden Rule

Treat Kids With Respect And They Will Respect You

Respect your children, and they will respect you. *boy 18*

Getting -really- angry doesn't help anyone. *girl 17*

Don't put down what your children do, support them 100% in their activities. *girl 14*

Respect. Nothing beats it, consider your child as an adult, and never pretend/show that you know more about them because one day they'll embarrass you. *boy 15*

Kids make mistakes so don't get mad when they mess up. *boy 16*

Treat kids with respect and they will respect you. *boy 16*

If your child is having a problem, ask them and if they want to be alone, then leave them alone. *girl 12*

Don't tell them that you hate them. *boy 15*

If a child wants a candy bar or something small like that, you should get it for him/her. Us kids do know you parents buy little things for yourself when we are not around. *girl 11*

The first thing you should do is make sure your child knows you are his/her friend. Try to have a good relationship. That really affects a good family. *girl 11*

Don't wear those "I'm with stupid ——-> " shirts. *girl 11*

Don't yell at anyone (well maybe a little.) *girl 11*

Do good deeds for each other. *boy 10*

If you don't agree talk it over quietly and politely. Fighting about it will only create a bigger mess. *girl 11*

Do not argue of strange matters. *girl 10*

Don't turn your child into a slave, hit them, or yell at them. *boy 11*

Do not yell at your children, talk nicely and calmly. *boy 13*

The last thing you should do when your kid tells you something bad is yell. That doesn't make them want to tell you anything. *girl 12*

Be nice, not mean but just nice like not to be hard on your kids. *boy 13*

Never ever hit your kid because that will just cause your kids to hit their kids. *boy 13*

Never hit. I personally have parents that don't hit and I respect that. Parents who hit their children are afraid. *girl 13*

Try not to yell. Being yelled at is scary. The disappointment thing is better, it makes you feel terrible. *girl 13*

Treat their children with the same respect they want their kids to have towards them. *girl 13*

Don't get mad at your child when they tell you they want to do drugs because if you yell at them they probably will. *girl 13*

Don't yell too much...just explain and talk. *girl 11*

Don't say so much, we hear you! *boy 12*

Don't yell at the top of your lungs, most kids are very sensitive. *boy 12*

If your children break something, don't yell until they admit who did it, and try not to yell much. *boy 12*

Don't get mad if we do something non-smart. *boy 12*

All of us are different and you can't compare us because it just hurts us. *girl 12*

Never beat or hit your child, That is a very big sin. Your child is a human, not a rag doll or a punching bag. If you know someone that is beating a child, call a local child abuse hotline. *girl 14*

Talk to your kids, don't yell. Trust me, it doesn't help. *girl 12*

Treat your parents like friends instead of enemies. *girl 12*

Don't yell at me if something is wrong, just tell me to correct what is wrong. *boy 11*

They should do a thing where we get to boss the parents around so they know what it feels like. *boy 12*

Don't yell at them for the way they are or what kind of music they listen to or the way they dress. *girl 12*

Don't call them names. *girl 12*

Don't curse and call your children names. *boy 13*

Don't push the whole family to not fight. You can ask, but don't push it too far because then they will avoid each other, plus the best part is making up. *boy 13*

Don't make people feel stupid, dumb, or like an idiot. *girl 13*

Don't have fights every 4 months. *girl 12*

Treat them with the same respect you would like to be treated.. Don't say "I'm the parent, you're the kid" that just makes us mad. *girl 14*

Don't threaten your children. *girl 14*

Most of all don't insult them. *girl 13*

Don't scream at your children too much or they won't listen to you.. They block it out and miss the important stuff. *girl 15*

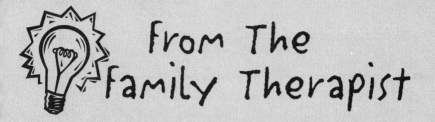

From The Family Therapist

Do you get the feeling after reading these comments that parental yelling and screaming doesn't really bring out the best in kids?

Again and again, the kids are saying variations of "Please don't hurt us." "Please treat us right." "We don't want to hurt you and we want to treat you right."

A parent-child relationship built upon mutual and healthy respect is the very best condition under which teens can grow into mentally and emotionally healthy adults.

I remember one family whose father was always finding fault with his children, never giving them the respect that they deserved.

The daughter became a lovely young woman, very pretty but a little bit plump. On her wedding day, supposedly one of the happiest and most joyous days of our lives, just as her father was about to walk her down the aisle, I heard him loudly say, "You look so fat in that dress." As if that wasn't bad enough to say in front of the guests, he went on to comment, "You better grow up fast and be a good wife, another husband will be hard to find for someone like you."

No doubt that twenty-something woman felt exactly the same as our 13-year-old commentator who said, "Don't make people feel stupid, dumb, or like an idiot."

Every culture since the beginning of time has believed in the moral truism, "We should treat others in the way we would like to be treated." Respect me and I will respect you.

That's basically what our teens here are suggesting and, as a family therapist, I wholeheartedly agree.

Dr. Carol's Tips on Mutual Respect

- It doesn't matter what else you do. If we don't respect ourselves… then we cannot respect our children nor they us.
- Hold your child in high esteem. Speak to them in ways that allow them to recognize that they are worthy of respect. Yelling isn't one of those ways.
- Respect them out of love…not out of a sense of duty. They will reciprocate.
- Think of respect as something to be earned…not demanded.
- The more you can help them respect themselves, the better chance they have of making good choices. If they don't believe they are worthy of anything, they will treat themselves and everyone around them accordingly.

Chapter 11
God and Morality

Teach Them So They Know What's Bad... and What's Good

No family will work without God. So really I would start with Him first. *girl 14*

You should talk to them about your experiences, so they know what's bad and what's good. *girl 12*

Take them to church and teach them about God. I sometimes am tempted to lie, disobey, or deceive my parents but my conscience is too big to ignore and I owe all that conscience to my mother and father for teaching me right and wrong. *girl 14*

You should bring your child to church a lot so that he/she has a good heart. *girl 15*

Make God the centerpiece of your family. *boy 18*

Pray with them a lot. *boy 17*

Encourage good habits to make them a better person. *boy 16*

Do what is right. *boy 12*

Another very important thing is going to church. I think church is a good place to go if you have any problems and it is a good place to be able to spend time with them. *girl 12*

Always pray together and say the rosary. *boy 11*

Try to pray and read stories with your family. *girl 11*

Pray together, it brings you together. *boy 11*

Teach your children to believe in God and not to be mean, hateful, or rude to others. *girl 11*

Be a good example to your children; teach them to follow the way of Jesus, because He is the Way, the Truth, and the Life. *girl 14*

Teach your children from the beginning about your faith. Catholics should raise their children to love Jesus and respect Him in the Eucharist. *girl 19*

Say prayers with them at night always! *girl 13*

Pray together because we need help from God. God listens to anything. *boy 13*

You should always pray together. *boy 13*

Work and pray together as a family. *girl 13*

Teach what is right and wrong. *girl 12*

A family will never, never be happy without God. It will never work. Now with God doesn't mean your family will be perfect and always happy. He lets you fall to be stronger. But it is always awesome to be able to go to a perfect God when you are upset. *girl 14*

Listen to Jesus…do what He says. *boy 17*

Live each day as if it were your last. *girl 13*

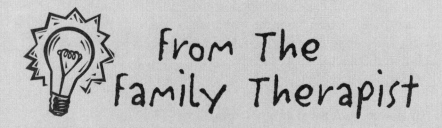
From The Family Therapist

I have found that the happiest, most content, and peaceful kids (as well as adults) are those that recognize that they are not the center of the universe. In fact, a real sense of life's importance comes to those who recognize that there is something greater than self.

The best gift we can give our children is helping them to realize the Love of God. We can only give it...if we have it. We can only raise moral kids if we teach them to think of themselves as sacred gifts... rather than as objects.

Morality has become such a loaded word in our culture. But it's simply based upon two principles: love and respect. It's a system for loving and respecting others and ourselves so that our choices do not violate our love and respect for each other.

In response to hot button issues like school shootings, teen pregnancies, and drugs...many point to the schools and demand that they start teaching morality.

But the public schools can teach only what's legal, what's illegal, what's a felony, and what's a misdemeanor. It's up to parents to teach "right" and "wrong."

It's up to parents to teach, share, and behave in accordance with the moral fiber and value system of the family. There can be no question in our children's minds that their family is built on a greater love that stretches far beyond the boundaries of their home.

Praying together and performing acts of community service together are wonderful steppingstones to fully appreciate the wonders of God.

Dr. Carol's Tips on Spirituality

- Pray together before everyone leaves for school and work. If you are uncomfortable praying aloud, take one minute of silent prayer. Pray together each night as well.

- Plan a service project together and bring it to completion.
- Worship together as a family each week. Spend time sharing together about the weekly message.
- Do it all in love. Don't just teach about a loving God, live it out at home.

Chapter 12

Discipline

Set Boundaries; Don't Let Your Children Do Just Anything.

Have consequences for your kids in case they get in trouble.
boy 11

We may hate punishment, but we need it, not too mean though. Example: don't punish for small things like spilling.
boy 13

Do not solve all your children's problems for them, but do not abandon them to flounder alone in the world. *girl 19*

Give your children freedom, but still enforce your rules.
girl 19

Stop bugging me about cleaning my room (it is my own problem if it is dirty.) *girl 13*

No comparing me to what my sisters would have done and how much better they did. *girl 13*

Stick by what you say. *girl 13*

Discipline them when they need it. *boy 14*

Do not, if you have more than one child, under any circumstances, compare the two kids. I have got an older brother, and though my parents try very hard not to compare us (and succeed 99.8% of the time) it's hard enough not to get depressed from his accomplishments by just living with him and hearing others talk. *girl 14*

And...I don't know, um, don't push too hard, always congratulate your kids even if they do bad, tell them they were great for trying. *boy 15*

Punish your children only when necessary, try being their friend once in a while (TRUST ME IT WILL HELP.) *girl 16*

Don't ground your kids for experimenting with smoking and alcohol. Tell them your experiences and let them make their own decision. If you tell them it is bad and never even try it, then your kids will rebel and do it, trust me I have friends to prove it. *girl 14*

More rules do NOT equal "better" behavior. *boy 18*

Please don't rip the covers off the bed on the school mornings in the middle of winter. It's cold. *boy 17*

Don't be judgmental; let your children dress and look like they want to. Don't discriminate against your child and their friends because of their appearance or because they may look weird, after all, it's not what it is on the outside that matters. *boy 14*

Set boundaries; don't let your children do just anything. Be lenient, but have a say in your child's activities. *girl 18*

Don't compare them with another kid. *boy 15*

Don't "baby" the youngest kid. *girl 12*

Parents should make it fair between them and their children and if they are angry they might let it out in school with weapons. *girl 13*

Don't pressure children into not doing something because they might do what they are not supposed to do. *girl 12*

A big thing is making brother or sisters get along and treating all the kids equally, you can't make brothers and sisters never fight but try to stop it a little and always spend an equal amount of time each and every child. *girl 12*

Parents shouldn't give in no matter how much the kids want something (I mean if it were dangerous.) *girl 11*

Set rules and don't waive them because we will assume you will do it again. *girl 14*

One of the most important things you need for a happy family is discipline. Do not be afraid to establish respect. Otherwise your children will walk all over you. If your child doesn't think you are the boss they will walk all over you and that's not a happy family. *girl 14*

Make bed times but make it like 15 minutes later each year on their birthday. *girl 14*

Don't ground the bigger brother for hitting the little sister for being a brat. *boy 13*

If you keep your kids locked up that they can't do anything and you are strict on them. I think that then the kids want to do bad stuff. *girl 11*

Let your kids learn from their mistakes and don't make your favorite words "no", "no way", and "never." *girl 12*

They should never treat their children differently; they should all get the same amount of love and attention as the others. *girl 11*

Don't compare us with our siblings. If they are better in school than we are, talk to them privately. *girl 11*

Don't let your children stay out until 2 in morning because they will be up getting in trouble. *boy 12*

When you come to a disagreement with your child, sit down and talk it out. Try not to raise your voice, because if you do, the child might try to compete with you by yelling back at you, and that will just cause a bigger conflict. *girl 14*

Remember who's the boss. You're the adult. *girl 14*

If they show they are angry or upset or talk to you in a manner you don't approve of or do something you don't approve of let them tell you what's wrong or if there is anything else that might have happened during the day that set them off before you just ground them. *girl 14*

Discipline them. I think discipline is very important even though I hate it when it is me being disciplined. I think that after talking to your kids (and listening) about what happened if they need to be disciplined, discipline them. *girl 14*

If they make one major mistake don't base the rest of their life on it or bring it up every time they do something wrong. *girl 14*

Never punish your kid by ignoring them. They will feel unloved and hurt. *girl 14*

You can give your kids chores; just don't go nuts, especially if you only have one child. *girl 12*

You should not be so demanding. If you want me to get something and I refuse, don't punish me just get it yourself. *boy 11*

When my dad was a teenager, he had about 8 dirt bikes. My dad only bought a golf cart and it is my sister's. *boy 12*

Try not to let your kids cuss or make them pay .10 cents each time. *girl 12*

Do things without your parents having to tell you a million times. *girl 12*

Don't bribe your kids for good grades. *girl 12*

Don't spoil the kids and wait on them, but don't make them do little things you can do like shut the cabinets. *girl 12*

Even though you kids don't like it, make rules. *boy 13*

If you spank them they will hurt animals and people. *girl 13*

Don't discipline them in public. *boy 13*

Make sure their punishment is fair for the disobedient behavior. *boy 13*

Be flexible with your decisions, let them have fun, but be stern when necessary. *boy 13*

Learn how to "say no." *boy 12*

If you have a fight try to resolve it and not wait it out. It will leave a scar if you do. *girl 13*

Discipline your kids. They will respect you more. *boy 13*

From The Family Therapist

Wow, listen to the kids. They WANT discipline. They want boundaries. They want rules, and they want to know the rules, so that they can better understand the game.

There are so many modern myths about teens. Many parents think that kids don't want rules and actually rationalize that they are doing their children a favor by not disciplining them.

Many Baby Boomer parents seem to almost cringe at the word, "discipline". They seek their children's love and affection by trying to be their children's friends.

As you can see in almost all of the quotes, children actually WANT boundaries. They want a safe predictable home, not chaos or anarchy.

Many parents come to me for family counseling demanding blind obedience from their children. The irony is that blind obedience is not something you want to instill in a teenager unless your objective is to raise a blindly obedient adult. Part of a child's natural development is the need to explore boundaries.

As parents, we want to raise children who have been taught "critical thinking" skills. It's very simple. Set boundaries and set consequences. Teach them simple logic. If you step outside the boundaries, then there will be consequences.

I am often asked by parents to suggest specific consequences. The truth is that every child is different. For some children, being sent alone to their room is a pleasure. For other teens, it's a very effective deterrent.

I suggest that you get your child's input on consequences. Most of the time, they will be very honest and let you know what will motivate them to stay within the boundaries.

For example, if your child is on a sports team and just lives to play that sport, then an effective consequence of seriously breaching the rules would be to be grounded from practice for a week. Disallowing telephone time with friends is an appropriate and effective consequence for most girls.

It is important to allow them to recognize that it is their choice. You are not punishing them. They made a choice when they chose the inappropriate behavior. Life is about good and bad choices and the good and bad consequences that those choices bring. Run a red light and possible consequences include getting a ticket or killing someone. Stay out past curfew and expect a consequence of losing phone privileges. Make a decision to study extra hard and bear the consequence of getting an "A". Make a decision to do a community service project and face the natural consequence of feeling good about oneself.

The simple point, and the children make it so well, is that discipline means setting appropriate boundaries and ensuring that predictable and fair consequences will result if the boundaries are crossed.

Dr. Carol's Tips For Establishing Consequences

- NEVER remove love. No matter what your child ever does, don't withhold your love for him or her. Some parents use love as a weapon. Strive to give unconditional love.
- Never use corporal punishment. But if your child steps out of line, just whack him or her across the head. Just kidding folks, corporal punishment simply creates more problems than it solves.
- DON'T verbally abuse your children. Some parents think that condemning, horrible words are an appropriate consequence when their child inevitably steps outside boundaries. It isn't. Be dispassionate. Deal with your anger. Count to ten if you have to. Deal with your child intelligently and compassionately. Set consequences in advance. Condemning negative words leave gaping wounds.

- Make the punishment fit the crime. As one child said, "Don't punish us for spilling things."
- Consequences should have a specific timeframe. Avoid open-ended consequences like, "You will never be allowed to do xyz again." If possible, give your child a way to eventually earn back whatever it is they have lost. The idea of redemption is a wonderful, hopeful thing.
- Stay calm. You already set the consequence, no need to repeat it.
- Don't ever tell your kids you will never trust them again.

Chapter 13

Freedom and Boundaries

Yes, They Will Make Mistakes, But Everybody Does! Even You Did.

Try not to interfere with the teenager's life too much. *boy 17*

The more you push your kids the more they will rebel. *girl 16*

Be a "cool " parent. Don't let them do EVERYTHING, but don't let them do nothing either. *boy 11*

Let them make their own mistakes even though you don't want them to get hurt. We need the life experiences. *girl 15*

Don't criticize all the time; some good comments go a long the way. *boy 16*

Don't try to control your teenager's life. They're not 2 years old anymore. *girl 13*

Don't bug them for unnecessary information, it leads to conflicts and can make the child keep to themselves even further (Nosiness.) *boy 14*

Let them grow up but don't get carried away. *girl 12*

Let your child feel safe where he or she belongs but don't let her/he feel so safe that she/he won't know how to solve their own problems. *girl 12*

Let them make choices on their own like trust and let them get things like Nintendo 64 and a dog*boy 12*

Try to be your child's friend, but don't forget that you are the parent. *girl 18*

Be strict, but flexible, more flexible as you get older. *girl 16*

If the parents just flat out says no boyfriends or girlfriends, then your child will just shut you out and keep on seeing that person. *girl 13*

Don't spend too much time with them. *boy 14*

Give more work to the oldest kid. *girl 12*

If they have done everything they had to do, let them go where ever they want and let them go out on weekends, they have only two days. *boy 13*

Don't push your kids too much but want them to do their best. *boy 12*

Let them be a little dangerous. *girl 10*

Give them a free rein and see where it takes them if they know you are always there to back them up or to comfort them. *girl 14*

Don't be afraid to let go. When your child wants to go out, to the movies maybe, let them go but be sure you know what movie they are seeing, but don't hover. *girl 14*

Let them sleep as late as they want, don't wake them up. *boy 14*

Be reasonable, we feel like we are almost grown adults, but only when we do something wrong...we are still kids. *boy 12*

Try to be your child's friend, but not his/her best friend.
boy 13

Give your kid freedom. Yes, they will make mistakes, but everybody does! Even you did. They will learn more from their mistakes than sitting at home and doing nothing. *girl 13*

Give them as much freedom as possible without shutting them out of your lives. *girl 13*

Let your children have a good social life. If they don't have good friends they will be miserable. Let them spend time with their friends. *girl 12*

Respect your child's right to close their door and be alone.
boy 12

We should be allowed to be home on Saturdays. *girl 13*

Your rooms do not have to be cleaned 24/7. *girl 13*

Don't criticize their clothes, hair, or friends unless they're acting like they are on drugs. *girl 13*

Let kids do dumb things like dying their hair and stuff, don't say no to that. *girl 12*

Give us money for no reason. *boy 13*

Whenever they want something, don't say no right away. *boy 13*

Times have changed; don't stick to ALL of your old principals. *boy 13*

Don't ask them constantly if they are a virgin. *girl 13*

Make them feel special, but don't spoil them. Every once in a while buy them a gift. *girl 13*

If it's not a big deal don't make one of it. *boy 14*

From The Family Therapist

One of the most important responsibilities for parents of teens is to teach their children to make good decisions.

It's a tough call for a parent to decide upon appropriate boundaries. Draw the reins in too tightly and there is a risk of stunting the child's critical thinking skills. Give the child too much slack and, in today's world, he or she might make a mistake that could be fatal.

Children, like everyone else in this world, are looking for that balance between freedom and responsibility.

Boundaries should be firm yet flexible. There is no one set of boundaries that will serve all children in all families. The parent is well served to keep in mind that the overall strategy, the goal, is to safely and lovingly raise a child so that he or she might become a responsible adult.

Rather than teaching details, the strategy ought to be to teach responsibility and critical thinking skills.

The trick is to encourage rather than push. Our priority should be to encourage our children's dreams and aspirations. Often parents turn dreams into negatives. For example, "How can you be an astronaut if you don't get an "A"?

Dr. Carol's Tips on Boundaries

- Set age-appropriate boundaries. There are several good books on this.
- From the early ages, teach your children to make good decisions. For example, give them choices regarding what to wear starting at an early age.
- Involve kids in chores, planning, and family decisions. One long-term study found that kids who feel like they contributed to the family grow into young adulthood feeling good about themselves.
- Provide a weekly list of chores, but let the kids choose when to do it. Of course, if a chore doesn't get done in the allotted time, there will be a consequence. For example, a policy that chores have to be complete by Saturday at 6 PM is much better than screaming "Clean your room right now" as you walk in the door.
- Actively involve teens in menu planning. Give them the responsibility to plan the menu one or two evenings per week.

- Encourage them to play chess and other strategy games that involve or require critical thinking skills. In chess, there is no luck involved and every move has consequences…good or bad. Encourage anything that requires them to *think things through* whether games, family discussions or planning.
- Get your child's input on boundaries and consequences.
- Instead of being a disciplinarian, teach your children to develop self-discipline by encouraging their good healthy choices and helping them understand when their choices are inappropriate.
- As you give your child an opportunity to develop critical thinking skills, you will feel more comfortable with your child's decision-making, which allows for more balance.
- Smile a lot. Don't take everything so seriously; it can get easier if you are not so tense.

Chapter 14

Acceptance and Understanding

Try And Understand Things From The Teenager's Point Of View.

Don't get real annoyed if your kid does something annoying.
girl 12

Try and understand things from the teenager's point of view.
boy 17

Let your kids make their own mistakes. *girl 16*

Always have an open mind about what they are saying, just because they are younger than you doesn't mean they aren't on the same level of intelligence as you. *girl 16*

Try to remember what you would have done in your kids' position. *girl 14*

Don't give them "when I was your age" BS speeches. *boy 18*

You did bad staff too when you were a kid.... You turned out fine, didn't you? *boy 18*

Accept the child's decisions of what they want to be either academically, sexually and mentally. *boy 16*

Try to realize, that sometimes you make mistakes too, and it's not always the child's fault. Even though they are younger and inexperienced,, they can be right in certain situations. *girl 14*

Kids are kids. They do forget some things you tell them; so don't give them too much to do. *girl 13*

When your children get older, they need an understanding friend, more than a parent. Listen and advise, but if you push, you might lose them. *girl 16*

Try to understand your children more. (ask questions) *girl 15*

Don't tell them to do all these things, they get lost. *boy 11*

I think that a parent should try to remember how it is to be a teenager and then to compromise...I think it would lead to a fun family. *girl 11*

Don't think that your kids are the only kids in the world that fight and don't get along. *girl 14*

Try to put yourself in everyone's position, if there's a fight, see it from both points of view...other people will appreciate you. *girl 13*

Don't give too many lectures, we actually hear you the first time you say one. *girl 13*

Think of how you wanted your life to be as a kid. Did you compare yourself to others on how to look or act? *girl 12*

Try to go with fads, don't be dorky. *girl 12*

We like to be known as adults, not babies. We like to be on our own...don't feel hurt. *girl 12*

Being is not always easy...we have to go through tough things too. *girl 12*

Never tell a child something to do or think if it is for 30 year olds. *girl 11*

When my dad was my age he always used to do bad things, but his parents didn't do anything. When I am bad I get grounded or yelled at. *boy 12*

I am sure that when my mom was a kid she did not like it when her mom yelled at her. When my mom yells at me it makes me feel bad. I guess she forgot how it feels. *boy 12*

We are younger than you and don't like to stay in all day. *boy 13*

Understanding... When you have a disagreement listen to what your kids, listen to what they say instead of telling them to listen to you instead of them listening to your yelling. *girl 14*

We're kids and we will eventually get on your nerves so take it easy. *boy 14*

Parents should remember how they felt when their parents said that they couldn't do something with friends. *girl 14*

And last but not least kids will be kids just like the saying when the cat is away the mice will play. Just don't be too rough on them. Remember back when you were a child and you wanted to have fun too. *girl 16*

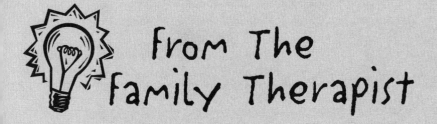

From The Family Therapist

The brain of a thirteen-year-old human is not the same as that of an adult. They don't think the same. They do not process information the same way that adults do and they should not be thought of as mini-adults.

Kids know this. They know that their parents do not understand them. Kids are wired differently than adults and, yes, it is hard for us parents to remember back to the way we used to think.

The priorities of kids are way different than the priorities of their parents. For example, many parents complain that their kids either don't do their chores or do them incompletely. They tend to forget that the kids live in a completely different world. They have a point of view that is very different than an adult point of view. They are wrapped up with their friends and they are quite self-absorbed. Yes, the secret is out. Most teens are self-absorbed...but don't worry, they will grow out of themselves just like you did.

Parents would do well to accept that very few kids live outside of the here and now. We have to accept that kids aren't usually thinking of their long-term future but are more worried about what they are going to do with their friends today.

I am NOT suggesting that parents accept bad behavior. I am suggesting that parents love and accept their kids where they are at, even while they set boundaries and consequences in the here and now.

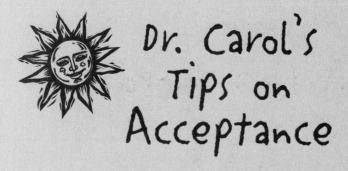

Dr. Carol's Tips on Acceptance

- Remember, accept and understand your son or daughter...you don't have to accept their behavior.
- Remind your children, as often as possible, that you regard them as cherished gifts.
- Remember that that children can sometimes feel like outcasts and victims at school. Make your home into a place where children feel especially accepted and wanted.
- Instead of putting your energy into trying to shape the "perfect" child....put all of your energy, every ounce of it, into trying to shape yourself into the very best parent that you can be.

Chapter 15

A Final Word

The news is great. Teens want a happy and fulfilling family life just like you do.

There's great hope even if you already have teens and things aren't going as well as everyone in the family would like. I am reminded of the wonderful, hopeful expression, "It's never too late to start over your day."

I urge parents to share this book with their children. Use each chapter heading as the basis for discussion. Pay particular attention to listening and communications skills. Start today. You already know parenting is the hardest thing that you will ever do. You also already know that it's the most fulfilling and worthwhile thing you will ever do. So don't ever give up!

Each chapter subheading was taken from a teen's comment. Here they are for your ready reference:

1. **Listen**
   With Your Mind, Heart, And Soul

2. **Talk To Your Kids!**
   They usually actually are listening, despite what you may think.

3. **Spend Time Together**
   Every Step Of The Way... Be There!

4. Play With Us
    At times just go and do fun things and
    forget about being a parent

5. Love
    Always love them....and harder.

6. Do As I Say, Not As I Do
    Always Lead By Example...Not By Dictatorship.

7. Ritual
    Eat Dinner Together.

8. Trust
    Trust The Job You Have Done With Us, Let Us
    Make And Learn From Our Mistakes.

9. Teach Your Children
    Help Them Achieve Things That Cannot Be
    Achieved Without a Parent's Help.

10. Respect: The Golden Rule
    Treat Kids With Respect And They Will
    Respect You.

11. God and Morality
    Teach Them So They Know What's Bad...
    and What's Good.

12. Discipline
    Set Boundaries; Don't Let Your Children
    Do Just Anything.

13. Freedom and Boundaries
    Yes, They Will Make Mistakes,
    But Everybody Does! Even You Did.

14. Acceptance and Understanding
    Try And Understand Things From
    The Teenager's Point Of View.

About the Authors

Dr. Carol Razza is a licensed family therapist of 20 years with a thriving family counseling practice in Wellington, Florida. She received an Ed.D. in Child and Youth Studies and a M.A. in Counseling Psychology from Nova University. Dr. Razza conducts frequent workshops and seminars on effective parenting skills. She has served as an Adjunct Professor at Palm Beach Community College and at St. Vincent De Paul Catholic seminary. She is the author of the book *FAMILY PLAY*, published by Eric Education Resources in 1994 and is the co-author of *SON-BLOCK*, published in 2001 by Clear Light Communications. Happily married to husband Paul for some 30 years, they have two children, Paul and Timothy.

Denis Eirikis is an award-winning freelance writer with three adolescent children. He and his wife own Clear Light Communications Inc., a publishing, marketing and public relations firm that works with a variety of major nonprofit organizations and corporations. Mr. Eirikis has a B.A. from St Thomas University, has served as a Commissioned US Coast Guard Officer, worked in some 46 countries as an oil company executive (before children), and is happily married for 17 years to his incredibly beautiful and patient wife Leonor. They live in Royal Palm Beach, FL with their three children: Mark, Steven, and Juliet Marie.

This is the co-authors' second book together. Clear Light Communications Inc publishes their book *SONBLOCK*.

Speaking Engagements

Dr. Carol Razza has a very active retreat and seminar ministry. If you would like to inquire about her speaking to your organization, please contact her office directly at 561/795-9724.

If you would like to learn more about her upcoming speaking schedule, please check out

www.clearlightcoms.com/drcarol

About the Cover Art

Daniel Fortune drew the wonderful depiction of the family on our book cover. Daniel, 17, was winner of a national art contest that drew a tremendous response from a wide variety of teenagers. Daniel is a Junior at Santaluces High School and plays on their school basketball team in Lantana, Florida. His hope is to one day become a professional graphic artist.

Thanks to Art Director Lyssa Z. Moody for incorporating Daniel's art into her design of the front and back cover of PARENT ME...PLEASE!

We regret that we are unable to acknowledge all the teens who entered the art contest, but we would like to make HONORABLE MENTION to the following entrants whose entries were particularly noteworthy:

Nour Saleh	Rafael Silva
Angela Spina	Eric Hawrykiun
Joe Craig	Rachel Leveille
Jair Salazar	Gabriel Merced
Sarah Bidmead	Juliet Marie Eirikis
Veronica Rodriguez	Monica Neelands

Also By Dr. Carol Razza and Denis Eirikis

SONBLOCK

How Christians Unknowingly Shield Themselves From Grace

"Your soul is solar powered. It runs on only one
thing...grace. It always thirsts. You can try feeding that
deep yearning inside with sex, alcohol, power or material
wealth...but these things can be more toxic than nutritious.
The soul craves only one thing...God's Light."

SONBLOCK explores defenses that people build in vain
attempts to fill themselves or to protect themselves from
hurt. Unfortunately, these defenses, like so much armor,
also tend to block people off from God and from each
other. Peppered with anecdotes from her 20 years
experience as a Licensed Family Therapist, the reader is
invited to explore and ask God for help with:

Loneliness of Distrust	**Mind Traps**
Armored Hearts	**Soul Sickness**
Toxic Unforgiveness	**Family Tree**
Fear and Anxiety	**Spiritual Poverty**

Order Hotline: 561/793-5222
www.clearlightcoms.com

Parents:

Hopefully, this book gave you a glimpse into the point of view of your adolescent or teen. One great way to start a new dialog with your son or daughter is to ask them to jot down five pieces of advice that they would give to any parents who want to raise a happy family. Their answers might surprise you and may even open the door to new and productive avenues of communication with your child.

If you want to share your child's wisdom with the world, then send their advice to:

Clear Light Communications Inc.
PARENT ME...PLEASE!
254 Las Palmas Street
Royal Palm Beach, FL 33411

or email parentme@clearlightcoms.com

Your child's response may be published anonymously in the next edition of Parent Me...Please!